BLESSED
to be Your
DOG

Celebrate the Stories of Your Fur Hero

A GUIDED JOURNAL

JEAN M. ALFIERI

BLESSED TO BE YOUR DOG

© Jean M. Alfieri

For information about special discounts available for bulk purchases, sales promotions, fund-raising and educational needs, please contact the author via email at: Jean@BlessedtobeMe.com

www.BlessedtobeMe.com

Interior and Cover Design by Christine Sterling-Bortner
Original Artwork by Alexandra Ruiz
Quotes designed by Christine Sterling-Bortner
Images licensed from Adobe Stock (www.stock.adobe.com)

IBSN PRINT: 978-1-7343086-1-7

Celebrating the Stories of

_____

Dedication

Thank YOU! – To everyone who requested this book. I thought I was the only one who wanted a dedicated place to capture all the funny, quirky, crazy antics of my dogs. Our pets are such a significant part of our lives. They share our sorrows and our joys. Their presence marks a certain era, leaving pawprints on our hearts.

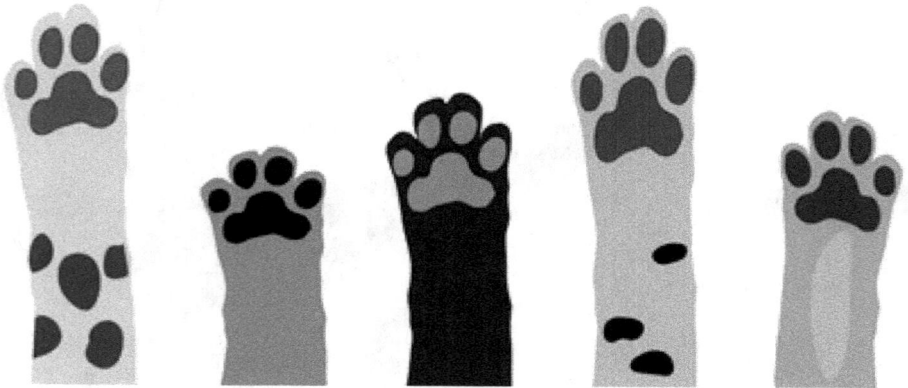

Introduction

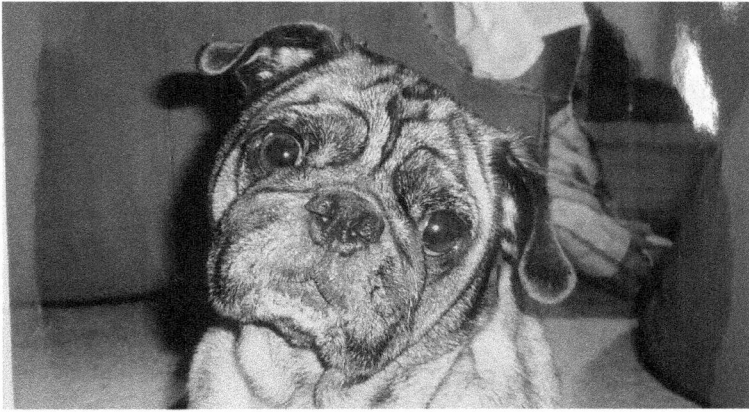

His name was Wyatt. A small dog, who filled the room with his big, boisterous personality. Wyatt picked me. No doubt about it. I had gone to the Humane Society looking for a specific breed -- not his. Yet, he sat proudly in the passenger seat next to me on our way home. A twenty-five-pound chunk of loveable pug! His tongue bobbed from his mouth. Eyes squinting as the cool A/C hit his face. Occasionally he would gaze out the window to take in the desert view. More frequently he looked at me, with an unmistakable admiration I knew was misplaced. He'd tilt his head as if saying, "Hello Hooman." To which I was compelled to reply, "Hello Pug."

That started an almost ten-year dialogue between Wyatt and I. Our terms of endearment quickly grew, and Wyatt was a great listener. He heard all about how my fiancé and I had called off our engagement. I was sad, but Wyatt made me smile -- as he did when he greeted my new boyfriend who would turn out to be my husband. I smiled all the more over his excitement when we packed up the house and moved from Arizona to Colorado, Wyatt on my lap the entire drive. It was quite a decade.

When he died, I was devastated. He brought so much joy and laughter to my life. The thought of our great adventures possibly being forgotten made my heartache even worse. To fend off the blues, I started journaling our fabulous memories. I cried, but it felt good, somehow therapeutic. That started a new journey. There is nothing that can replace Wyatt's beautiful spirit but writing about his silly, sweet, and stubborn personality helped me mend.

I wish I had started journaling about Wyatt years earlier, but no matter the age of your dog, I encourage you to make this book your own. Capture the stories while they're fresh. Enjoy and embrace all the blessings you share.

YOUR BLESSINGS

Proud to be Your Hooman
(Stories from the Fur-parent)

Proud to be Your Pup
(Stories from the Fur-kid)

HOW TO USE THIS BOOK

Each "Blessing" section will include a prompt to jog the memories you choose to document. Your writing should be as short or long as you want. If the prompt doesn't exactly fit your story but reminds you of a different fabulous story, write that one! The tone, texture and spin are all you — and your dog. Embrace the look back at your real-life adventures.

"Blessed to be Your Dog" will:
- Allow you to explore and reflect
- Prompt you to capture your fondest memories
- Provide space to celebrate and honor your special relationship
- Guide you in composing a treasured keepsake

You will find hints and suggestions offered with each Blessing. These are an assortment of ideas, from which you can pick and choose. Use what you like. Leave what you don't. There are no boundaries. This project is all about individual style. It's designed to capture the memories that make you smile. Allow yourself to savor it.

Disclaimer – some of the Blessings are written in present tense while others are offered in past tense. This is by design. Please capture your stories in whichever tense is right for you. It matters not where your dog is physically, only that you hold them close in your heart.

Start wherever you are most comfortable -- at the beginning, or flip through the pages until you land on a special subject. Enjoy the writing journey. When you've completed each prompt, you will have captured fourteen wonderful memories, and possibly more! You may be surprised at what you discover.

PROUD TO BE YOUR HOOMAN

(Stories from the Fur-parent)

This section captures your (human) point-of-view. Journal as you typically would; including your own insights and stories.

Blessing #1

PUPPY LOVE

(IT'S NOT AN AGE,
BUT A MINDSET!)

Maybe your dog was a just a little ball of fur when you first met. Maybe your eyes caught those of an older pup you rescued. Something made you choose THAT dog – or did they choose you?

Capture the story of how this precious canine came into your life. On the next pages, remember the details through the questions presented. There is extra space where you can write out special memories!

1. WHERE AND HOW DID YOU MEET?

....
....
....
....

2. WAS ANYONE ELSE THERE?

....
....
....
....

3. HOW WAS YOUR PUP NAMED, AND WHY DID THAT NAME FIT SO WELL?

....
....
....
....

4. WHAT DID YOUR DOG DO WHEN YOU FIRST TOUCHED,
   HELD, PET HER/HIM?

....

....

....

....

5. WHAT WAS UNIQUE ABOUT THIS DOG?

....

....

....

6. WHEN DID YOU KNOW THIS WAS A PERFECT FIT?

....

....

....

....

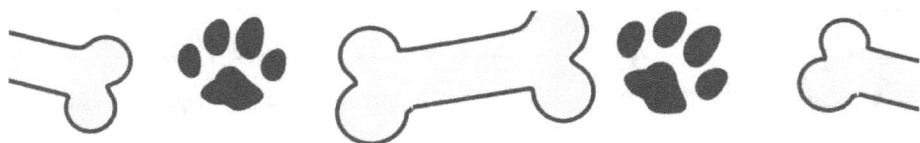

"It's just the most amazing thing to love a dog, isn't it? It makes our relationships with people seem as boring as a bowl of oatmeal."

— John Grogan

Blessing #2

No Place Like Home

Whether you are trampled as you walk in or a more sensible greeting awaits you, there is joy and anticipation in that wagging tail on the other side of the door.

What happens when you walk in? Complete chaos, or is your pup fast asleep? The dog's perspective is captured in the next section. This space is for you to share how it feels to return home to their company.

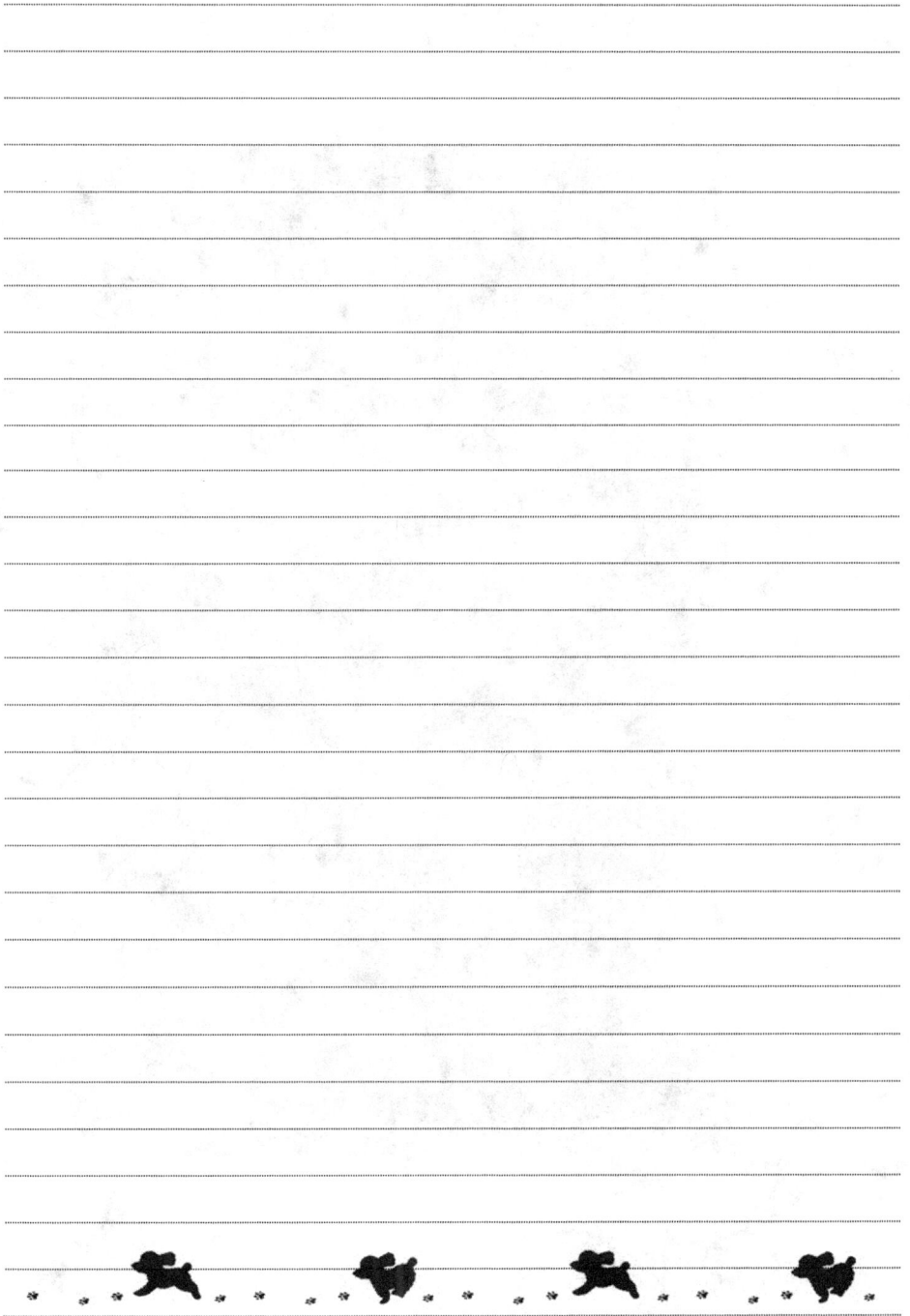

"IN TIMES OF JOY, ALL OF US WISHED WE POSSESSED A TAIL WE COULD WAG."
— W. H. AUDEN

Blessing #3

GRAND
ADVENTURES

Perhaps it was a once-in-a-lifetime vacation or an annual RV camping trip. It could have even been a more regular outing. Whether the destination was a routine trip to the pet store, a visit to a dog park, or a walk around the block, every outing was an opportunity for a grand adventure!

Consider these details:

- Where did your dog love to go?
- What / who was there?
- Why was that trip such fun?
- What did he/she do upon arrival?
- How long did you stay?

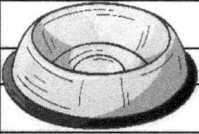

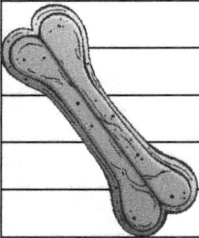

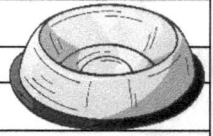

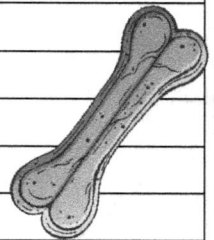

"Dogs feel very strongly that they should always go with you in the car, in case the need should arise for them to bark violently at nothing right in your ear."
— Dave Barry

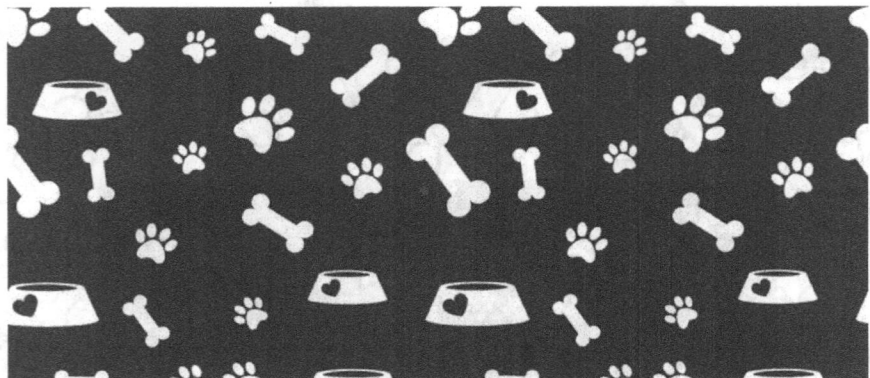

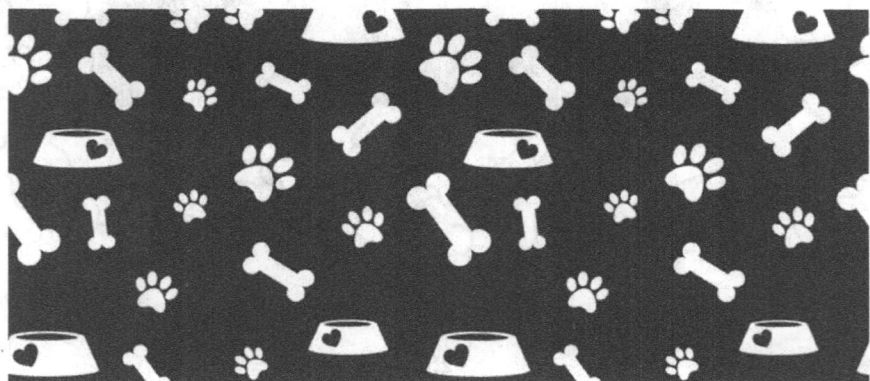

Blessing #4

PAW-TEE TIME

Recall a festive occasion to dress-up: a themed event or an especially hilarious Halloween costume ... as if not all dog costumes are hilarious! (This is a great place to include pictures!)

1. FAVORITE HOOMAN THAT VISITS / PARTIES WITH US:

_____

_____

_____

_____

2. WHAT WE DID ON YOUR BIRTHDAY/ADOPTION DAY:

_____

_____

_____

_____

3. WHAT WE DID ON MY BIRTHDAY:

_____

_____

_____

_____

4. I NEVER LAUGHED SO HARD AS WHEN:

_____

_____

_____

_____

5. OTHER SPECIAL OCCASIONS OR ANNUAL EVENTS WE CELEBRATE:

"IF YOU ARE A
DOG AND YOUR
OWNER SUGGESTS
THAT YOU WEAR A
SWEATER... SUGGEST
THAT HE WEAR A
TAIL."
- FRAN LEBOWITZ

Blessing #5

THE DOG DAZE

Special memories aren't always tied to special events. The best times are often ordinary days. Your dog wanders over and puts his head in your lap or (depending on size) curls up on it. It's the loving interruptions, the nudges, and the kisses, that make a day special.

1. THE THING YOU DO THAT ALWAYS MADE ME SMILE:

_____

_____

_____

_____

2. I WAS SOOOO PROUD OF YOU WHEN:

_____

_____

_____

_____

3. OUR MORNINGS ALWAYS START WITH:

_____

_____

_____

_____

4. OUR EVENINGS CLOSE WITH:

_____

_____

_____

_____

5. WHEN I LEAST EXPECT IT, YOU WILL:

....

....

....

....

6. YOU KNEW WHEN I WAS SAD OR UPSET BECAUSE YOU WOULD:

....

....

....

....

7. I LOVE THAT YOU LOVE NAPTIME. WE ALWAYS:

....

....

....

....

8. THE FUNNIEST / SWEETEST / BEST THING ABOUT YOU:

....

....

....

"The most affectionate creature in the world is a wet dog."
- Ambrose Bierce

WHAT FIVE WORDS WOULD BEST DESCRIBE YOUR DOG?

1

2

3

4

5

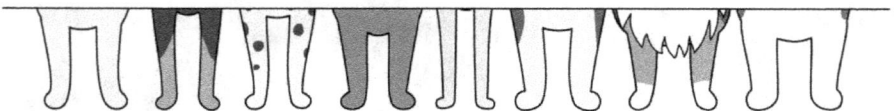

Blessing #6

MY FAVORITE STORY OF YOU

This dog was special in many ways, but there is one story that you find yourself telling whenever you talk about him/her. It captures the love, the humor, the joy -- the dogmanity of that precious spirit. It's a classic.

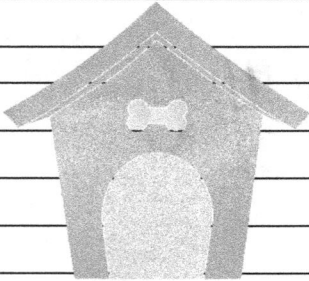

"ONCE YOU
HAVE HAD A
WONDERFUL
DOG, A LIFE
WITHOUT
ONE, IS A LIFE
DIMINISHED."
— DEAN KOONTZ

Blessing #7

SHARING THE LOVE

You know the grand times and special bond you've shared with your dog. It may be surprising to learn what fond memories others have of your pup, and just how much love that dog spread in their life. Ask and see!

Favorite story about your dog from a special friend/family member (or) what they adored most about your dog:

"Dogs' lives are too short. Their only fault, really."

— Agnes Sligh Turnbull

PROUD TO BE YOUR PUP

(Stories from the Fur-kid)

This section captures stories from YOUR DOG's point-of-view. After all, you know exactly what that pup is thinking. Have fun telling it in their own words!

Blessing #1

NICE TO MEET ME

🐾🐾🐾🐾🐾🐾

1. IT MAY HAVE TAKEN SOME ADJUSTING WHEN I GOT HOME, BUT I KNEW YOU LOVED ME WHEN:

_____
_____
_____
_____

🐾🐾🐾🐾🐾🐾

2. YOU KNEW I LOVED YOU WHEN:

_____
_____
_____
_____

🐾🐾🐾🐾🐾🐾

3. THANKS FOR TEACHING ME HOW TO:

_____
_____
_____
_____

🐾🐾🐾🐾🐾🐾

4. MY FAVORITE SHOW:

_____
_____
_____
_____

🐾🐾🐾🐾🐾🐾

5. MY FAVORITE SONG:

_____
_____
_____
_____

6. MY FAVORITE MOVIE:

_____
_____
_____
_____

7. MY FAVORITE CAR-TRIP DESTINATION:

_____
_____
_____
_____

8. OTHER FAVORITES:

_____
_____
_____
_____

9. I HAVE SOME AWESOME NICKNAMES, INCLUDING:

"Dogs do speak,
but only to those
who know how to
listen."

— Orhan Pamuk

Blessing #2

D-O-G
Spells
Trouble

✿ ✿ ✿ ✿ ✿ ✿ ✿ ✿ ✿ ✿ ✿ ✿ ✿ ✿ ✿ ✿ ✿ ✿ ✿

1. REMEMBER THAT THING I JUST COULDN'T RESIST? IT MAY HAVE BEEN A ONE-TIME OCCURRENCE, OR A CONSTANT PLAGUE. THAT THING WAS NOTHING LESS THAN A BATTLE OF WILLS.

2. I COULDN'T HELP IT WHEN:

3. WHEN I GET EXCITED, I SHOW IT BY:

4. I WOULD BEHAVE IF:

5. YOU TRIED NOT TO LAUGH, BUT I SAW YOU SMILE WHEN:

6. I LOVE TO CHEW ON:

7. I DIDN'T DO IT! IT WAS:

"After years of having a dog, you know him. You know the meaning of his snuffs and grunts and barks. Every twitch of the ears is a question or statement, every wag of the tail is an exclamation."
— Robert R. McCammon

Blessing #3

ALL
RUFFED-UP

1. I COULD DO THIS FOR DAYS IF YOU LET ME. YOU KNOW, THAT GOOFING-AROUND WE DO, THAT MAKES ME POUNCE AND PLAY AND GET ALL RILED UP.

2. GRRRRR! – I CAN'T STAND IT WHEN:

3. BUT I LOOOOOVE IT WHEN:

4. WHENEVER I GET A BATH:

5. UNMISTAKABLY ME! THAT SOUND I MAKE (A SNORT, A WHINE, A HOWL), OR THAT SILLY ANTIC I DO (A BUMP, A NOD, A NIBBLE) IT'S LIKE MY SIGNATURE.

6. I LOVE CHASING:

7. SOMETIMES THE JOURNEY WAS AS AWESOME AS THE DESTINATION! WHEN WE GO FOR A RIDE I ALWAYS:

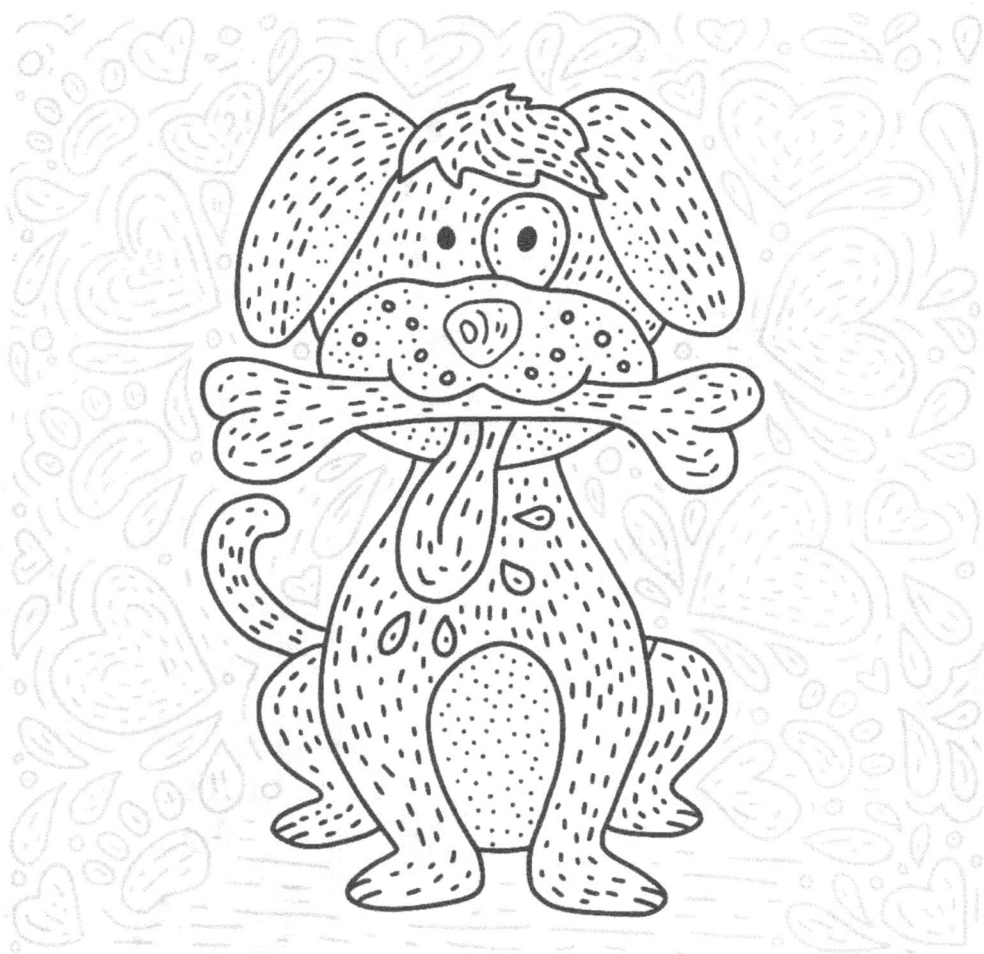

"I'M SUSPICIOUS OF PEOPLE WHO DON'T LIKE DOGS, BUT I TRUST A DOG WHEN IT DOESN'T LIKE A PERSON."
— BILL MURRAY

WHAT FIVE WORDS WOULD YOUR DOG USE TO DESCRIBE YOU?

1

2

3

4

5

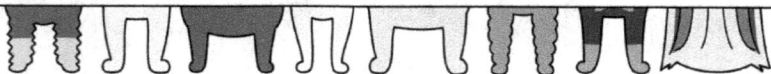

Blessing #4

THE HOWLIDAYS

We didn't need a calendar to make an occasion special. Where food and fun were involved, I was celebrating! If the doorbell rang, I was raising the woof! When you returned from being out of town for a couple days, well, let's not even go there!

1. MY FAVORITE DAY OF THE WEEK IS _____
   BECAUSE:
   _____
   _____
   _____
   _____

2. I LOVE TO BARK AT:
   _____
   _____
   _____

3. I LOVE TO PLAY WITH:
   _____
   _____
   _____

4. MY FAVORITE DAY OF THE YEAR IS _____
   BECAUSE:
   _____
   _____
   _____
   _____

5. MY FAVORITE DOG TREAT:

_____

_____

_____

_____

6. MY FAVORITE PEOPLE-TREAT:

_____

_____

_____

_____

7. MY FAVORITE PART OF EACH DAY IS _ _ _ _ _ _ _ _ _ _ _ _ _ _ BECAUSE:

_____

_____

_____

_____

8. IT WAS FUN WHEN WE:

_____

_____

_____

_____

"I care not for a man's religion whose dog and cat are not the better for it."

— Abraham Lincoln

A Picture is Worth a Thousand Words

Blessing #5

My (other) favorite Hoomans

Whether it's Grandma who lets me lick the bottom of the sour cream container, that friend who knows just how to scratch behind my ears, or my brother that gets down on the floor to play, these are the ones who make up my people-pack.

An honorable mention to those fur-friends who rank right up there with my hoomans!

YOU are the best, that goes without saying. We've got some cool friends and family too.

My list of favorites and what I love about them!

_____   BECAUSE:

_____ BECAUSE:

....

....

....

_____ BECAUSE:

....

....

....

_____ BECAUSE:

....

....

....

"THE AVERAGE DOG IS A NICER PERSON THAN THE AVERAGE PERSON."
— ANDY ROONEY

Blessing #6

No Place Like Home

I know you're home as soon as:

- 🦴
- 🦴
- 🦴
- 🦴
- 🦴

FIRST, I ....

THEN I ....

THEN WE ....

1. MY FAVORITE PLACE TO WATCH THE WORLD:

....
....
....
....

2. MY FAVORITE PLACE TO NAP:

_____

_____

_____

_____

3. THE BEST PART OF OUR WALKS IS:

_____

_____

_____

_____

4. MY FAVORITE THING IN THE MORNING:

_____

_____

_____

_____

5. MY FAVORITE THING ABOUT THE EVENING:

_____

_____

_____

_____

"THE DOG'S AGENDA IS SIMPLE, FATHOMABLE, OVERT: I WANT. (I WANT TO GO OUT, COME IN, EAT SOMETHING, LIE HERE, PLAY WITH THAT, KISS YOU.) THERE ARE NO ULTERIOR MOTIVES WITH A DOG, NO MIND GAMES, NO SECOND-GUESSING, NO COMPLICATED NEGOTIATIONS OR BARGAINS, AND NO GUILT TRIPS OR GRUDGES IF A REQUEST IS DENIED."
— CAROLINE KNAPP

Blessing #7

MY FAVORITE STORY

This one goes down in MY "all-time greatest" book! Was it that holiday mishap from which I benefited? Perhaps that time I caught you (or someone else) in a compromising moment? Or was it that impromptu contest between us of who could be sillier?

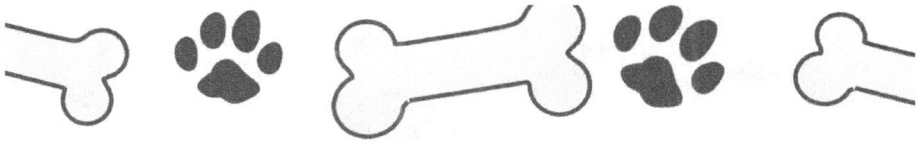

"The greatest pleasure of a dog is that you may make a fool of yourself with him, and not only will he not scold you, but he will make a fool of himself, too."
— Samuel Butler

Bonus Blessing

A Letter to Your Dog

Whether a short note or a longer message, what better way to convey your love and appreciation than in a letter to your dog? Consider what you adore most about this precious pup. Let the words come straight from your heart.

Additional Memories

WooF
DOG
WooF
DOG
WooF
DOG
WooF
DOG
WooF
DOG
DOG
DOG
WooF
DOG
WooF
DOG
DOG
WooF
WooF
WooF
DOG
WooF
DOG
WooF
DOG
WooF
DOG
WooF
DOG
WooF
DOG
DOG
DOG
WooF
DOG
WooF
DOG
DOG
WooF
WooF

I am your guardian. You are my hero. Though I try my best to show it, I can never thank you enough for picking me to be a part of your family. Though you may consider me a blessing, I could only enjoy this life because of you.

Thank you for remembering me.

"If there are no dogs in Heaven, then when I die, I want to go where they went."
— Will Rogers

About the Author

Jean knew when her eyes locked with those of a smooshy-faced little dog who sat inside a kennel at the Humane Society, that it was love at first sight. After almost a decade of making memories, it was a labor of love to self-publish a collection of short story poems starring her precious pug named "Zuggy", some years after he died. She wanted to ensure that her fondest memories with her beloved pet would not be forgotten. In doing this, Jean realized how much of our human legacy is lost within a single generation. Inspired, she created "Blessed to be Me" and "Blessed to be Your Dog", to celebrate the stories and special companions of your life.

A writer, speaker and dog-fan, Jean encourages others to capture and share their amazing stories in these guided journals. She offers presentations and workshops on the subject and enjoys visiting groups to offer others inspiration and support on their exciting and life-changing writing journey.

Jean is an avid proponent of adoption for all dogs: pure breeds, mixed breeds, young or "vintage" (her preference) who need a forever home. Her favorite breed is Rescued. She and her husband reside with their fur-family in Colorado Springs, Colorado. They often joke that although they pay the mortgage, the dogs own the house!

Find out more about Jean and her books at www.JeanAlfieri.com.

Acknowledgments

I am grateful to our Dear Lord, who has gifted me the opportunity to create this (and other) books. It's a dream many have but few fulfill. For His grace and provision, as I search for the right words. I pray that He infuses these pages with a spirit of peace, joy, and encouragement.

To my "tribe", without whose support and guidance, this book would still be a draft!

- CHRISTINE STERLING-BORTNER – for her coaching, cover and print-design, and layout expertise
- ACFW- CO SPRINGS CRITIQUE GROUP – for their always loving, constructive and honest feedback
- KAREN BARTA-BAIRD – for her keen eye and disciplined editing skills. Plus, she's not a schmucky friend!
- My husband, JOSH and our son, COLLIN – for welcoming and embracing all our four-legged fur-kids
- MOM, DAD, ANTH, PETE and JOANNE – for being my biggest cheerleaders

To the many vintage puppies who have blessed our lives (and I pray, the many more to come):

WYATT – Pug	CHANCE – Chow mix
RUMBLE – Doberman	DAISY – Airedale
DUKE – Airedale	MAX – Dachshund-Terrier mix
CONNER – Pug	REGGIE – Chihuahua
PRINCESS ZOEY – Pug	SILLY SALLY SUE – Airedale

SWEET LADY JANE – Boxer-Beagle mix
GAVIN – Chug (Chihuahua-Pug mix)

THE MORE I
LEARN ABOUT
PEOPLE, THE
MORE I LIKE
MY DOG.

- MARK TWAIN

www.ingramcontent.com/pod-product-compliance
Lightning Source LLC
Chambersburg PA
CBHW050550280326
41933CB00011B/1792